ANIMAL LIVES & LIFE CYCLES

Let's Investigate

by Ruth Owen and Victoria Dobney

Consultant:
Nicky Waller

Ruby Tuesday Books

Published in 2019 by Ruby Tuesday Books Ltd.

Editor: Mark J. Sachner
Designer: Emma Randall
Production: John Lingham

Photo credits:

Alamy: 8 (bottom), 24; FLPA: 5 (top), 16; Getty Images: 17 (top); Nature Picture Library: 20 (bottom left), 20 (bottom right); Hubert Polacek: 5 (centre); Shutterstock: Cover, 1, 2–3, 4, 6–7, 8 (top), 9 (top right), 9 (bottom), 10–11, 12–13, 14–15, 18–19, 20 (centre), 21, 22–23, 25, 26–27, 28–29; Superstock: 5 (bottom), 9 (top left), 17 (bottom); Warren Photographic: 20 (top).

ISBN 978-1-78856-033-7

Printed in China by Toppan Leefung Printing Limited

www.rubytuesdaybooks.com

Contents

The download button shows there are free worksheets or other resources available. Go to:
www.rubytuesdaybooks.com/scienceKS2

What Is an Animal?

Sharks, fleas, penguins, jellyfish, worms, humans – what have we all got in common? We are all animals.

What makes an animal an animal? The answer to that question is lots of things.

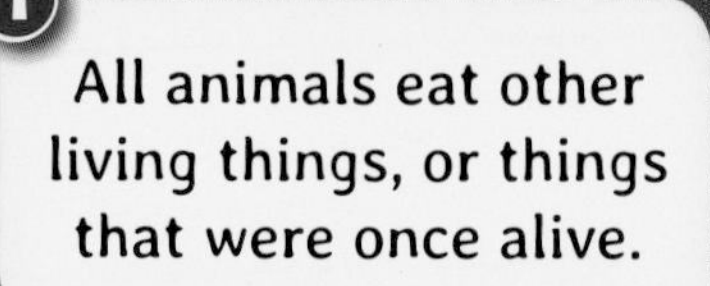

1. All animals eat other living things, or things that were once alive.

Designed For Fishing

A puffin can carry around 10 **fish** at once when it's gathering herrings or sand eels for its chick. Inside a puffin's beak there are tiny spines. The **bird**'s tongue pushes its catch onto the spines. With the fish safely pinned inside, the bird can then open its beak to catch more.

2. Almost all animals need to breathe, or take in, oxygen to survive.

Blowhole

Taking a Breath

Like all **mammals**, dolphins have lungs and must breathe oxygen from the air. To do this, a dolphin swims to the water's surface. Then it breathes by opening and closing the blowhole on top of its head.

Slime Motion

Slugs **secrete** slime from their whole bodies. The slime is made of water and glue-like substances. Some slime is thin and stops a slug's body from drying out. Other slime is thicker and helps a slug to slide over the ground or even cling to walls upside-down!

③ All animals are able to move around at some time in their lives.

④ All animals are able to **reproduce** and have young. Most animals need a **mate** to reproduce, but some female animals can go it alone.

Slime

Baby-Making Machines

Aphids are tiny **insects** that can reproduce by mating. However, females can also give birth to nymphs (young aphids) without mating. A female can produce nymphs when she's just a week old. She may live for about a month and give birth to five nymphs each day.

Nymph

Adult female aphid giving birth

Protective Mum!

A female American alligator buries her eggs in a nest made of sticks, leaves and mud. Then the **reptile** guards the nest from raccoons and other egg thieves. After about 60 days, her babies hatch and start squeaking. She digs the hatchlings from the mud and the tiny alligators crawl to the nearest water. Sometimes they even get a ride in mum's huge, toothy jaws!

All About Vertebrates

When we study living things, it is very helpful to classify, or sort, them into groups. Scientists divide animals into two large main groups – vertebrates and invertebrates.

All vertebrates have something in common.

Look at these images of vertebrates.
Can you spot something they all have?

(Turn your book upside-down for the answer.)

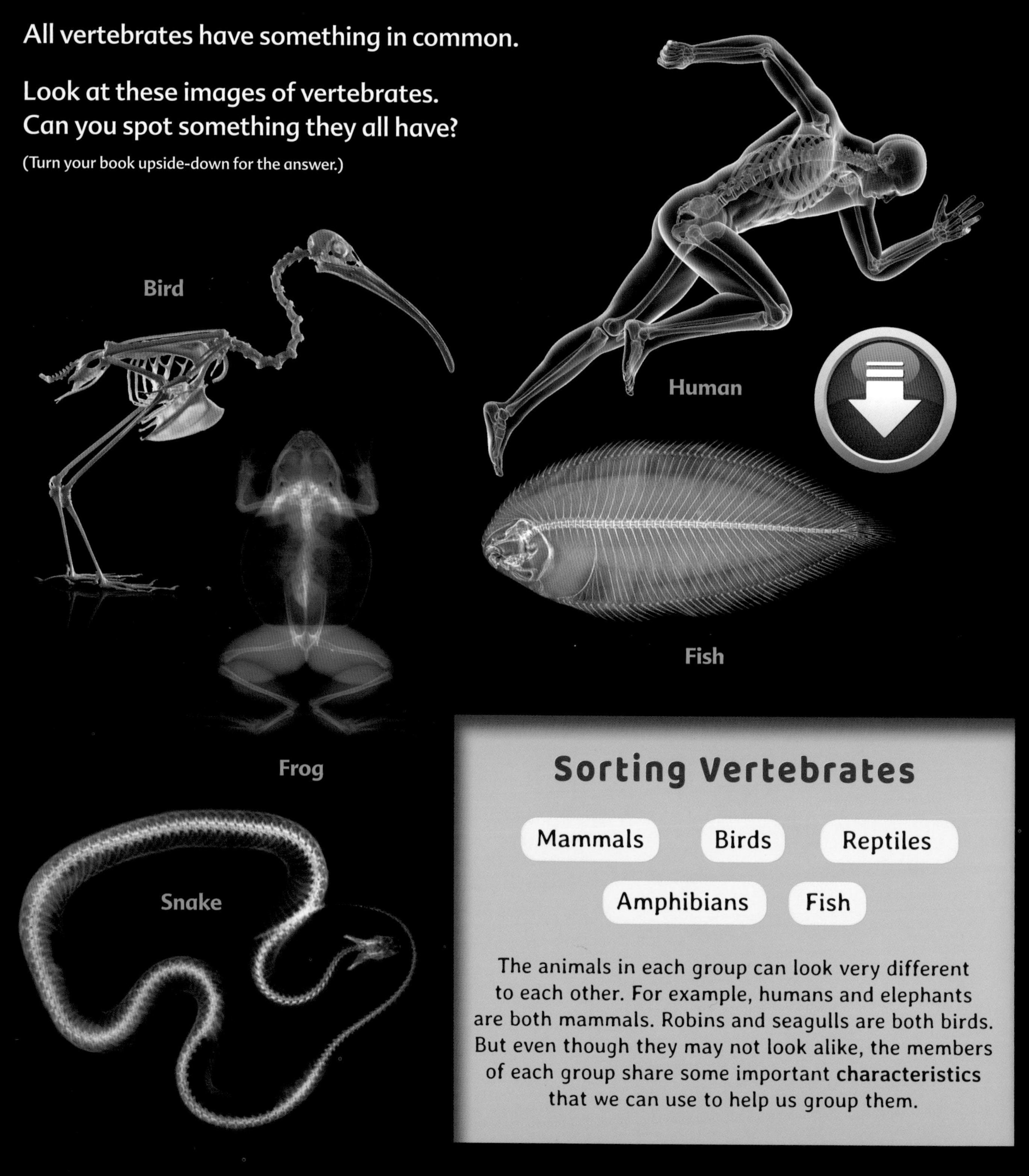

Sorting Vertebrates

Mammals

Birds

Reptiles

Amphibians

Fish

The animals in each group can look very different to each other. For example, humans and elephants are both mammals. Robins and seagulls are both birds. But even though they may not look alike, the members of each group share some important **characteristics** that we can use to help us group them.

All vertebrates have a backbone, or spine.
They also have other bones that form a skeleton inside their bodies.

Vertebrate Characteristics

Cold-blooded (or ectothermic) Animals that don't generate their own body heat. They get heat from the air or water around them.

Warm-blooded (or endothermic) Animals that can generate their own body heat.

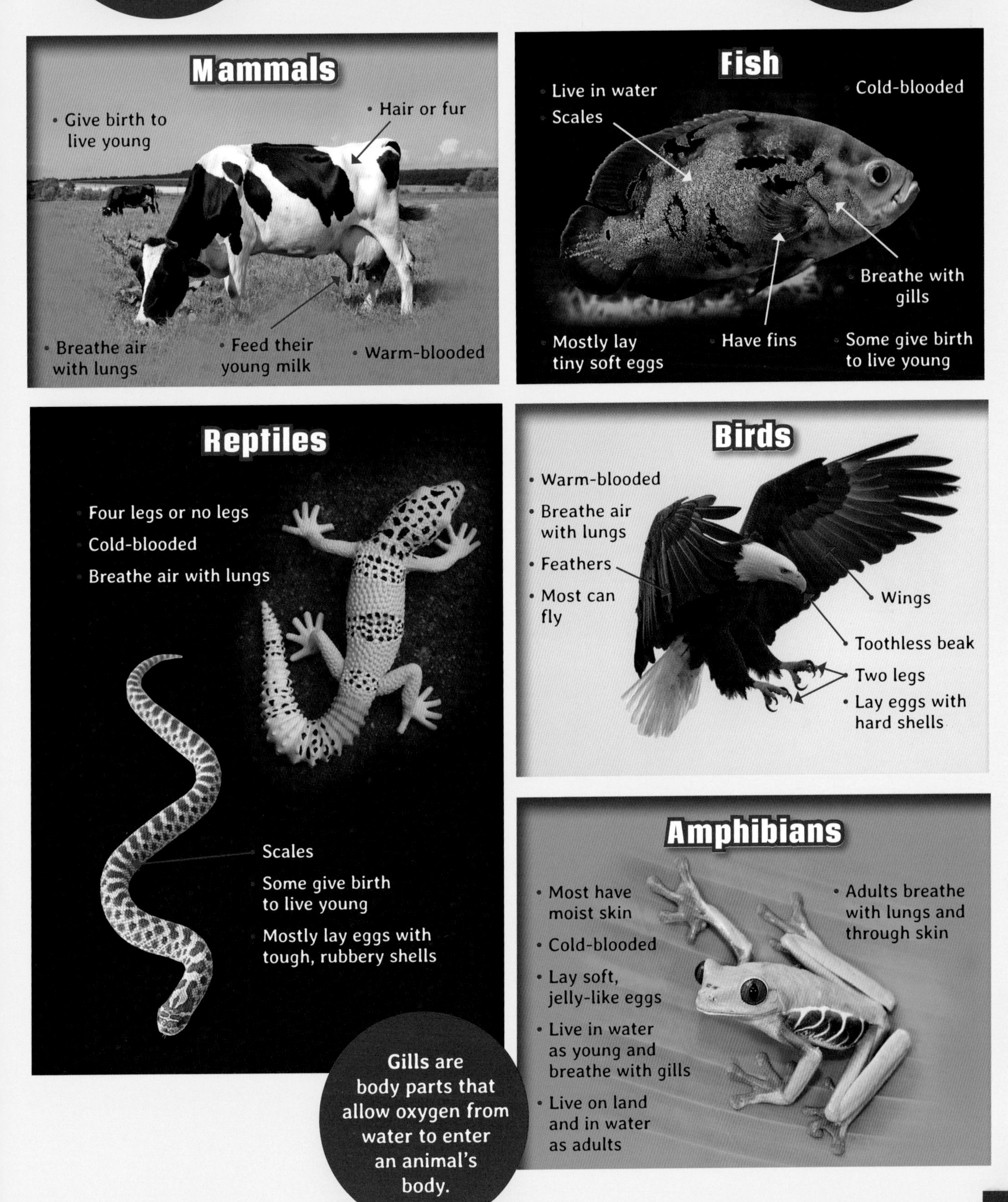

Gills are body parts that allow oxygen from water to enter an animal's body.

All About Invertebrates

Invertebrates are animals that do not have a backbone or any other bones.

Banded jewel beetle

Closed wing covers

Three pairs of legs

Most invertebrate animals, such as insects and **spiders**, have an **exoskeleton.** This tough shell is like a suit of armour on the outside of their soft bodies.

Insect Characteristics

- Six legs
- A body in three main parts: head, thorax, abdomen
- A pair of antennae for touching and smelling
- Most have wings

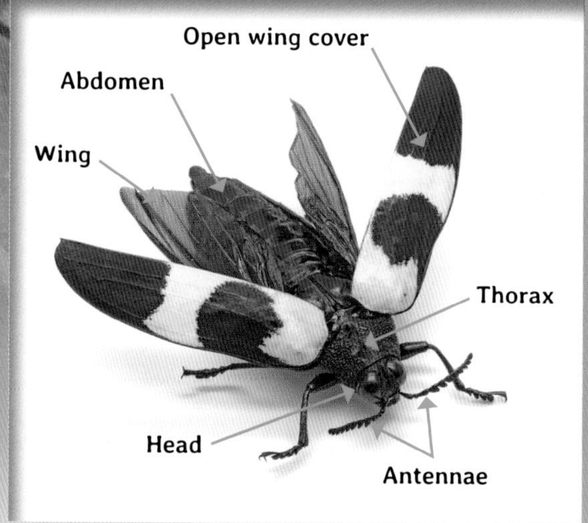

Spider Characteristics

- Eight legs
- A body in two main parts: abdomen and cephalothorax (which includes the head)
- A pair of chelicerae (jaws)
- A pair of pedipalps for tasting and smelling

New Armour

As a spider grows, its exoskeleton gets too tight. Eventually, it moults, or breaks out of, its old tight armour. Underneath there is a brand new exoskeleton!

Some invertebrates have no bones and no exoskeleton. These kinds of soft-bodied animals include worms, slugs, snails and ocean animals such as jellyfish and sea cucumbers.

No Legs, No Problem

An earthworm may be soft but it can still push through soil. It moves by stretching out the front part of its body. Then it pulls its tail end forward. Tiny, thorn-like hairs called setae cover the worm's skin. The setae grab the soil and help the worm move along.

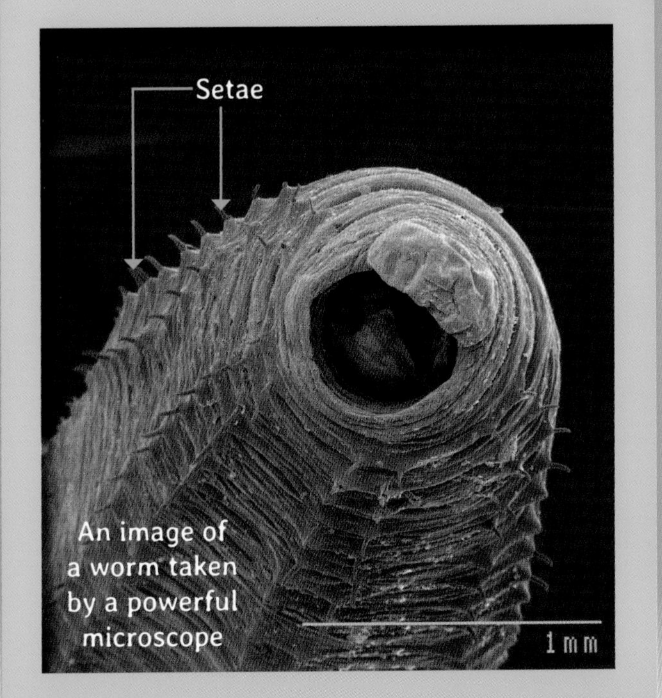

An image of a worm taken by a powerful microscope

Ocean Jellies

The lion's mane jellyfish gets its name from its hundreds of frothy, orange tentacles that look like a lion's mane. The tentacles can grow up to 30 metres long. The jellyfish captures fish and other small ocean creatures by stinging them with its tentacles.

The jellyfish's bell can be 2 metres across.

Spaghetti Attack!

It's called a sea cucumber, but it's actually an animal. When under attack from a **predator**, a sea cucumber shoots a mass of sticky, poisonous threads out of its anus (bottom). As the attacker struggles to break free from the threads, the slow-moving cucumber makes its escape.

What's on the Menu?

The kinds of foods animals eat help us to classify them into three large groups – carnivores, herbivores and omnivores. Their teeth and mouthparts can also help to show us what's on the menu.

Dust mite

Carnivores eat only meat.

- Some carnivores are predators that hunt live animals.
- Others scavenge on dead bodies.

Omnivores eat meat and plants.

- Humans are omnivores, but some people choose not to eat meat.

Herbivores eat only plants.

- Their foods include grass, twigs, leaves (including dead leaves) and **nectar**.

Let's Talk!

Dust mites are eight-legged relatives of spiders. What do you think these microscopic carnivores feed on?

(The answer is on page 32.)

Hunting with Whiskers

Walruses eat mussels, crabs, clams and worms. A walrus blasts water from its nostrils onto the seabed to stir up the sand. This disturbs the tiny animals that are hiding on the seabed. Then the big carnivorous mammal uses its sensitive whiskers to feel for any movements from its **prey**.

A walrus's moustache contains about 700 bristles, called vibrissae.

A Tongue for Nectar

A hummingbird hawk-moth gets its name because it hovers over flowers like a miniature hummingbird. It beats its wings so fast, they make a humming sound. The tiny herbivore drinks nectar through its long, tongue-like mouthpart called a proboscis.

Jaws x 2

The giant moray eel is a type of carnivorous fish. It hides in its cave until another fish swims by – then it attacks. The eel's teeth hook into its prey so the fish can't escape. Then a second set of jaws spring forward from inside the eel's throat and drag its victim down into its stomach!

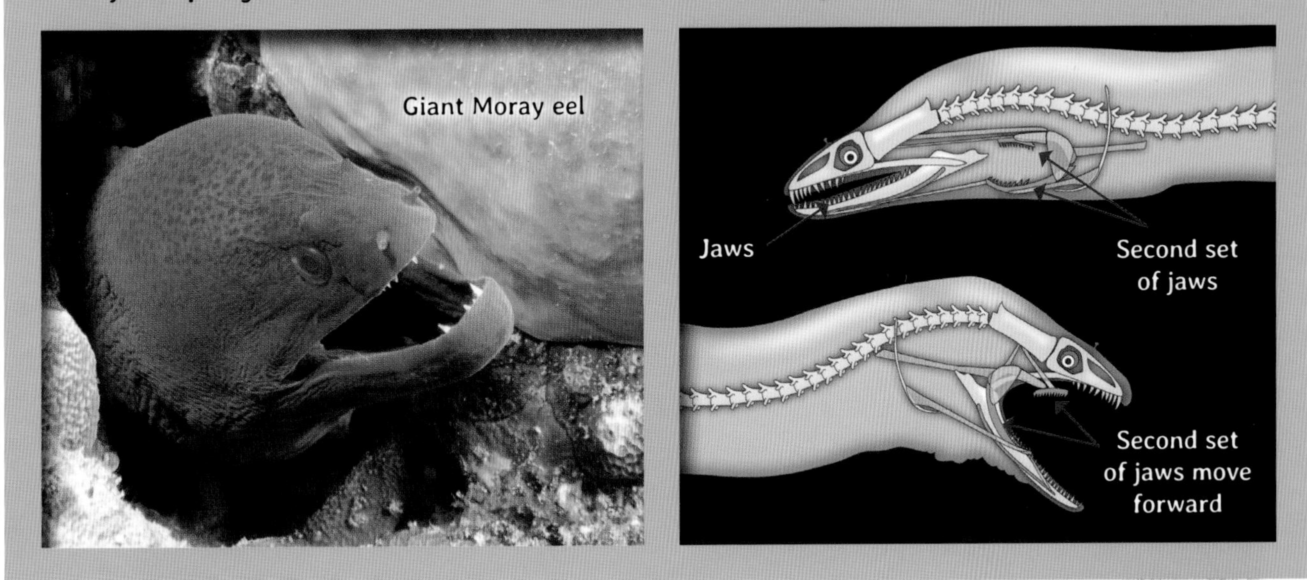

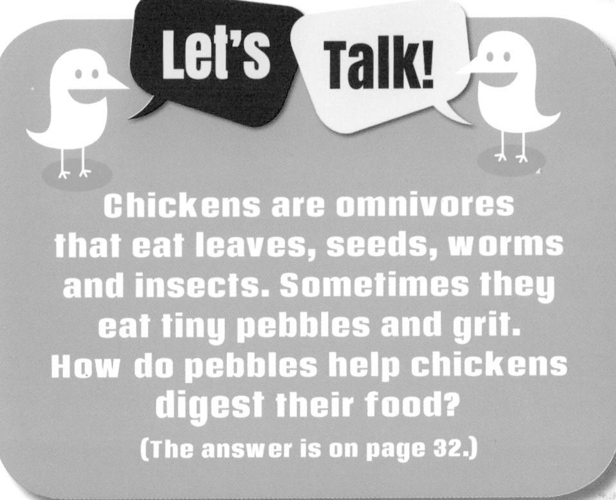

Chickens are omnivores that eat leaves, seeds, worms and insects. Sometimes they eat tiny pebbles and grit. How do pebbles help chickens digest their food?

(The answer is on page 32.)

Who Is Eating Who?

The living things in a natural habitat are all part of food chains and food webs. Let's investigate!

A food chain shows how plants and animals get their **energy**.

An oak tree is a **producer**. It gets its energy by producing its own sugary food in a process called **photosynthesis**. To do this, the plant needs sunlight.

The oak tree's wood, leaves and acorns are eaten by **consumers**. These are animals such as beetles, caterpillars and squirrels.

Oak tree

Acorns

In a woodland habitat, a tawny owl is a consumer. It's a predator that hunts for prey such as mice, frogs and small birds.

A Woodland Food Chain

All food chains begin with energy from the Sun and have a predator at the top.

The arrows mean "is eaten by" or "gives energy to".

Tawny owl

Oak tree

Sun

Mouse

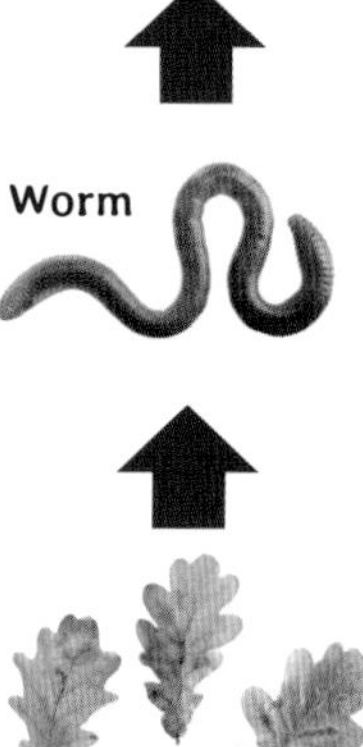

Sun

Some animals, like the mouse, can be prey and a predator.

Woodland Food Web

Plants and animals can belong to more than one food chain.

These different relationships can be shown as a food web.

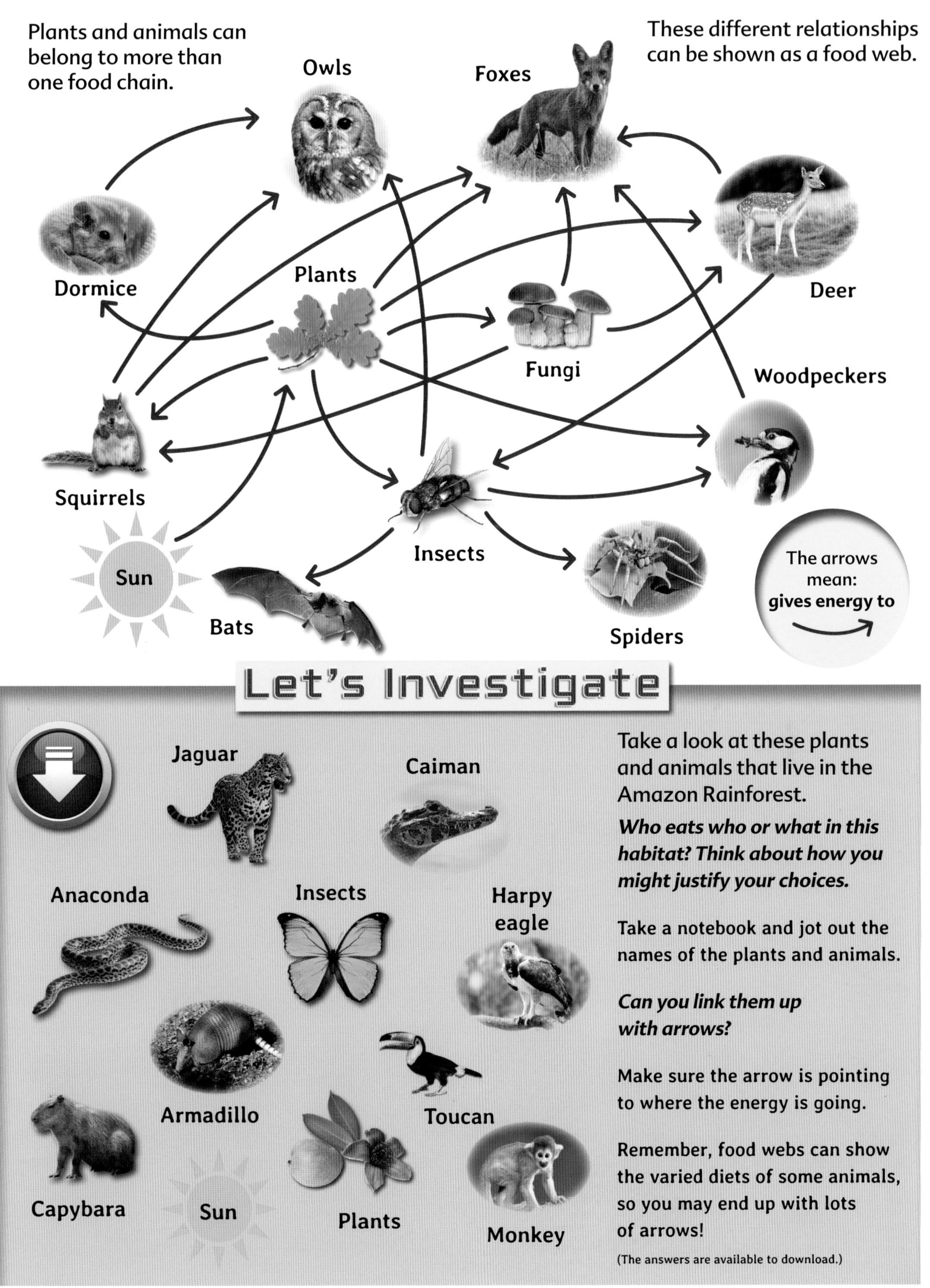

Let's Investigate

Take a look at these plants and animals that live in the Amazon Rainforest.

Who eats who or what in this habitat? Think about how you might justify your choices.

Take a notebook and jot out the names of the plants and animals.

Can you link them up with arrows?

Make sure the arrow is pointing to where the energy is going.

Remember, food webs can show the varied diets of some animals, so you may end up with lots of arrows!

(The answers are available to download.)

Classifying Animals

We've already discovered that living things can be classified, or grouped, in lots of different ways. But why is classifying animals important?

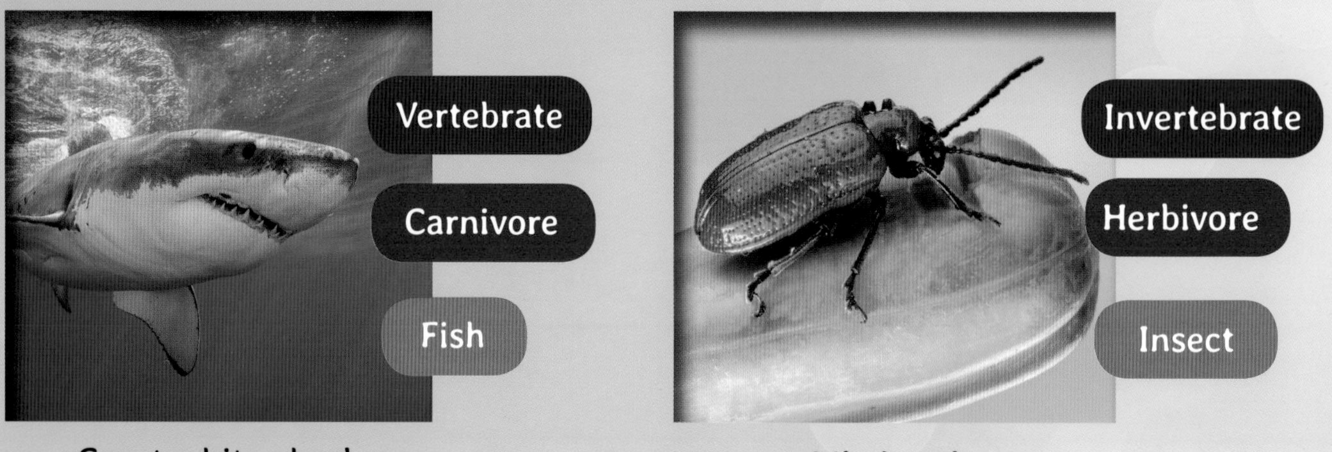

Great white shark
(Carcharodon carcharias)

Lily beetle
(Lilioceris lilii)

When a new animal is discovered, scientists can compare it to the animals in different classification groups. By comparing its characteristics to other animals, they can learn what kind of animal it is.

Carl Linnaeus: Classifying and Naming

One of the first people to use classification was a Swedish scientist named Carl Linnaeus. He created a systematic way to classify living things in the 1700s. We still use this system today. Linnaeus also invented a way to name living things called the binomial naming system. Under this system, every living thing is given a two-word Latin name. The first part is the genus (or group) name. The second word is the **species** name.

For example:

Panthera tigris = Tiger *Panthera leo* = Lion

Naming animals in this way makes it easier for scientists to communicate – even if they all speak different languages and have different words for tiger and lion.

Tiger
(Panthera tigris)

Lion
(Panthera Leo)

Jaguar
(Panthera onca)

Leopard
(Panthera pardus)

Classification Key

Classification Keys are used to sort things according to their characteristics. They are made up of questions with a "yes" or "no" answer. Have a go at sorting these butterflies and moths that you might find in your garden.

Method:

1. Choose an insect to classify and start with the first question at the top of the classification key.
2. Follow the branches for either "yes" or "no" and then ask yourself the next question.
3. When you have reached the last question, you will know what moth or butterfly you have chosen.

Now you have sorted these butterflies and moths, what features do you think might distinguish moths and butterflies?

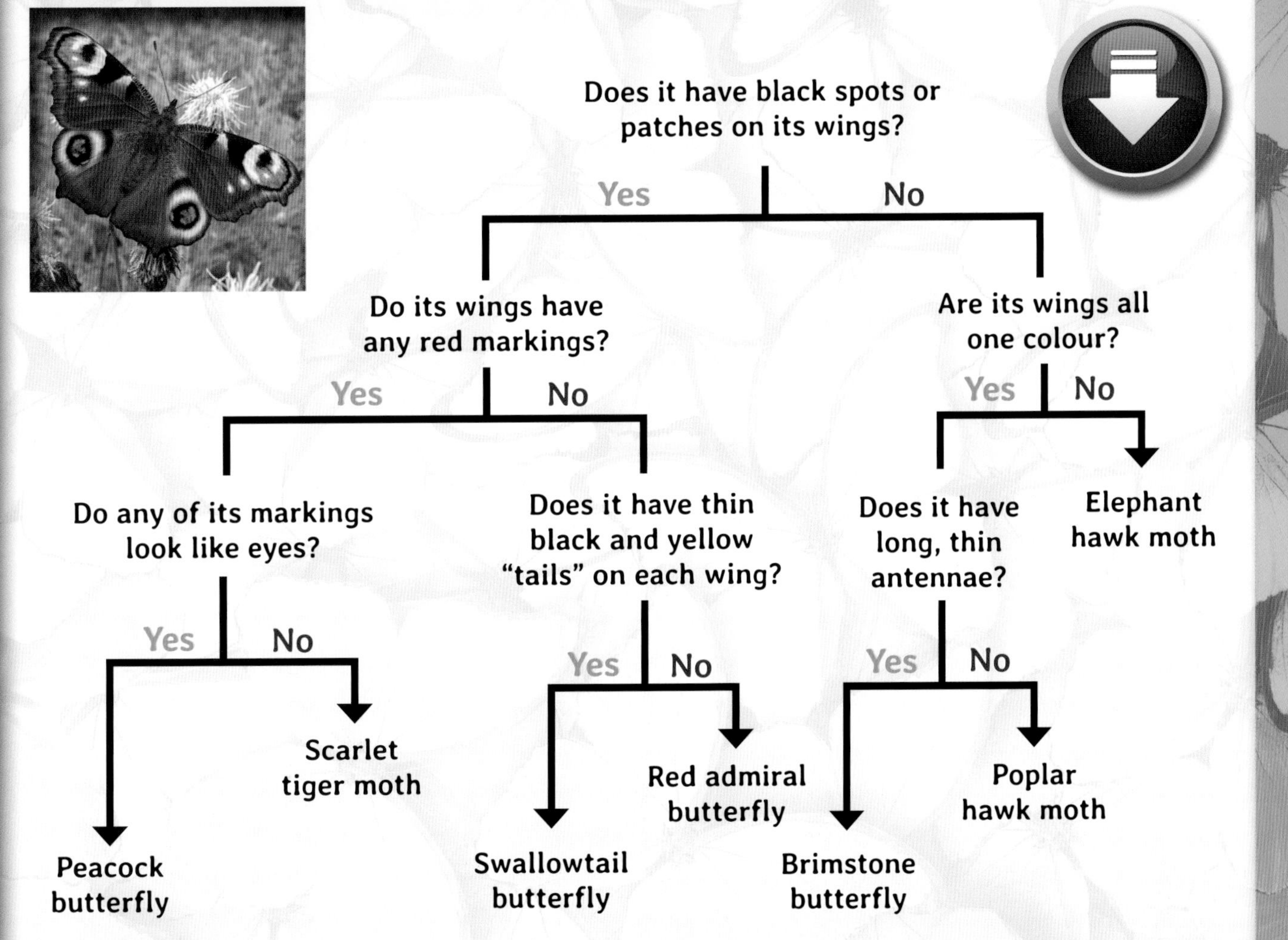

Mammal Life Cycle:

Blue Whale

Blue whales are the largest animals that have ever lived on Earth. Scientists believe that even during the Age of the Dinosaurs, no animal grew as big as these magnificent mammals.

Blue whales can grow to about 30 metres long and weigh around 180,000 kilograms – the weight of 30 elephants!

Adult blue whales sometimes live in small groups but often live alone.

When a female blue whale is about 10 years old, she is ready to mate. Males and females meet up to mate but do not stay together afterwards.

A blue whale is pregnant for about 12 months. Her calf is born underwater and must quickly swim to the surface to take its first breath.

A newborn blue whale is about 7 metres long and weighs 2000 to 4000 kilograms.

What is this weight similar to?

Let's Test It

Imagine your playground is the ocean. Measure out the length of an adult blue whale. How many children would weigh the same as the whale?

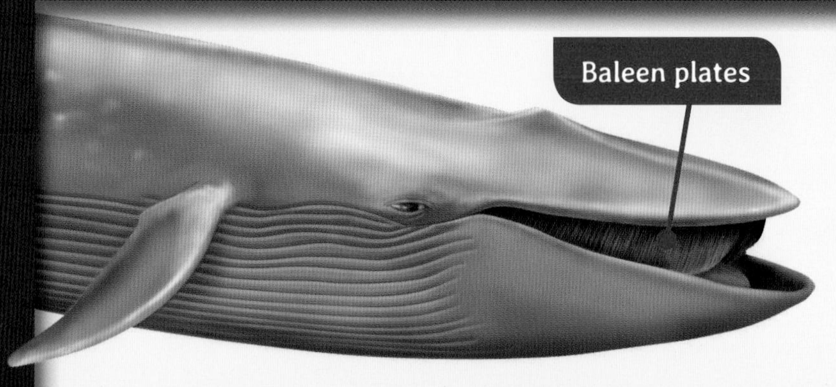

Big Eaters, Tiny Prey

Blue whales eat tiny shrimp-like animals called krill. To feed, a blue whale gulps up a huge mouthful of water. Its tongue pushes the water through fringe-like mouthparts called baleen plates. The krill get trapped in the plates and are swallowed by the whale. An adult whale can eat about 40 million krill in a day!

Each day, the calf drinks up to 500 litres of its mother's thick, fatty milk. It grows quickly, gaining about 90 kilograms in weight every day!

The calf drinks milk until it is about eight months old. Then, like its mother, it feeds on krill.

A blue whale calf lives with its mother for about a year. By this time it is about 15 metres long and ready to take care of itself.

Calf

Mother blue whale

Blue whales are endangered and scientists estimate there may only be 10,000 to 25,000 left around the world. Download an information sheet to learn all about the threats to blue whales.

When the young whale is six to 10 years old, it will be ready to reproduce. Scientists estimate that blue whales can live for up to 90 years.

Amphibian Life Cycle: Toad

Like most amphibians, toads spend part of their lives in water and part on land.

Adult toads like to live in damp, dark places. A toad's burrow might be under some rocks or inside a log pile or upturned flowerpot in a garden.

When a female toad is about four years old, she is ready to mate. In spring, she walks to a nearby pond.

Dozens and sometimes hundreds of toads may gather at a pond to mate.

Male toads are smaller than females.

The female toad jumps into the pond and meets a male toad.

The male clings to her back. As she lays her eggs, the male **fertilises** them with his sperm.

Female toad

A female toad lays about 5000 eggs under the water. The eggs are in long strings.

The female toad returns to her burrow and does not take care of her eggs or young.

After about 10 to 14 days, tiny tadpoles hatch from the toad's eggs. The tadpoles live underwater and breathe through gills.

Toad eggs floating in water

The tadpoles grow back legs and then front legs. Their tails get shorter and they start to form lungs for breathing air. When the tadpoles are about eight weeks old, they leave the pond. Now they are air-breathing toadlets that can live on land.

The tadpoles have long tails.

An eight-week-old toadlet is about 1.5 cm long.

It takes three to four years for a toadlet to grow into an adult toad. Toads can live for about nine years.

Insect Life Cycle:

Stag Beetle

Stag beetles are insects that spend most of their lives underground. They are Britain's largest beetle.

Beneath a dead tree stump in the dark, crumbly soil, fat white stag beetle **larvae** are hatching from their eggs.

A larva has mouthparts called mandibles that it uses to bite and chew wood.

When the larvae are hungry, they wriggle up into the tree stump and feed on the dead wood. The young insects live under the tree stump for about five years, growing bigger and bigger.

One day, each larva makes a **cocoon** around itself from soil and wood. This takes about two months.

Cocoon

Pupa

Inside its cocoon, the larva bursts out of its old exoskeleton and emerges as a **pupa**. Soon more changes start to take place. After about 35 days, the pupa's outer covering splits and underneath is the beetle's adult body.

The stag beetles dig up to the surface and start to look for mates.

Adult mandibles

Female stag beetle

An adult male stag beetle is 7 cm long.

A male stag beetle chooses an area to be his **territory** and mates with all the females in that area. If another male comes into his territory, there's a fight!

Once a female beetle has mated, she goes back to where she lived as a larva. She digs down into the soil and lays about 20 tiny white eggs.

The adult stag beetles live above ground for about six weeks and then they die.

But under the soil, tiny larvae are hatching and the cycle begins again!

Stag beetles fight with their mandibles until one gives in.

Let's Talk!

In what ways is a stag beetle's life cycle similar to a toad's? In what ways is it different?

Bird Life Cycle:

Swallow

It's April in the UK. A male and female swallow swoop and dive around a farmyard catching flies to eat. The birds have just returned from their winter migration to Africa.

Swallows often become mates for life.

The swallows gather beakfuls of mud from streams and ponds which they stick to the wall in an old barn. Beakful by beakful, they build their bowl-shaped nest. Then the female swallow lays five eggs in the nest.

The nest is lined with feathers, animal hair and soft grass. Each egg is about the size of a small grape.

The female **incubates** the eggs for 16 days until the chicks hatch. At first, the chicks are blind and have no feathers, but day by day they begin to look more like their parents.

The parent swallows bring the hungry chicks insects to eat.

10-day-old chick

After three weeks, the chicks are ready to **fledge**. The fledglings balance on the edge of the nest and practise flapping their wings. Finally, one by one they jump from the nest and make their first flights with their parents.

Mud nest

Fledgling

The chicks stay close to their parents for about a week. They learn to take care of themselves, but they still beg for food.

In August or September, it is time for the swallows to fly back to Africa, where it is warmer for the winter. But next spring they will return and this summer's chicks will be ready to raise families of their own.

A First Migration

It's not just the adult birds that make the six-week-long flight back to Africa. The young birds who hatched this summer will also go, flying about 320 kilometres each day!

Science in Action: Jane Goodall

Many scientists have dedicated their lives to studying and protecting wild animals. Some have changed the world of science forever!

Jane observing chimps at Gombe

Born in 1934, Jane Goodall grew up in a time when women were expected to be wives, mothers, nurses or, as Jane trained to be, secretaries. They certainly weren't supposed to be scientists. . . .

From a young age, Jane showed a keen interest in animals and she dreamed of working in the forests of Africa. This was an unusual ambition for a girl at this time.

In 1957, Jane got the chance to travel to Africa. In Kenya, she met scientist Louis Leakey. He originally hired Jane as an assistant. But then he invited her to study a group of chimpanzees with him in the Gombe Stream National Park, in Tanzania.

Instead of numbering the animals she studied (which was normal at the time), Jane gave them names. She didn't watch them from a distance but spent day after day getting closer to them, until they accepted her as one of their group.

During the 1960s, scientists believed that animals had limited intelligence and lacked personalities. Jane would soon make discoveries that challenged this.

Recording

Jane invented her own way of recording her scientific observations using notebooks and checklists.

A chimp using a tool (stick) to "fish" for food.

One day, while observing a chimpanzee she'd named David Greybeard, Jane noticed some behaviour that had never been seen before. David made a tool by taking the leaves off a stick. He then used the stick to catch and eat insects from a termite mound.

Jane also saw another chimp use a crumpled leaf as a bowl for drinking rainwater. These discoveries showed the world that humans weren't the only animals to use tools.

Observing

By carefully observing chimps and making detailed notes, Jane discovered that they share many emotions with humans. They comfort each other when they are unhappy. They kiss and hug and have deep family bonds. But when conflicts occur, they may fight and even kill their own kind – just as people do.

Conclusions

Until Jane's study, scientists believed that chimps were herbivores. Jane observed them hunting and eating monkeys, wild pigs and other small animals. She showed that chimps were in fact omnivores.

At first, some other scientists called Jane's methods of observing animals unscientific. However, they soon realised the importance of her discoveries. Today, many scientists use Jane's up-close way of studying wild animals.

Where Did Birds Come From?

There have been animals on Earth for millions and millions of years. Most animals from prehistoric times went extinct. But some evolved and became new kinds of animals that we see around us every day!

In 1861, **palaeontologists** in Germany found various **fossilised** remains of a crow-sized, bird-like creature. They named it *Archaeopteryx*.

Fingers with claws

Long tail bone

Wing

Archaeopteryx **fossil**

Archaeopteryx had sharp teeth and three fingers with claws on each of its wings. It lived about 150 million years ago – alongside the dinosaurs! Its name means "old wing".

Archaeopteryx may have looked like this.

Archaeopteryx was like a dinosaur because it had teeth and claws. But it had feathers and could fly like a bird.

By examining the newly discovered animal and comparing it to lots of dinosaur fossils, palaeontologists eventually discovered something amazing — birds evolved from dinosaurs!

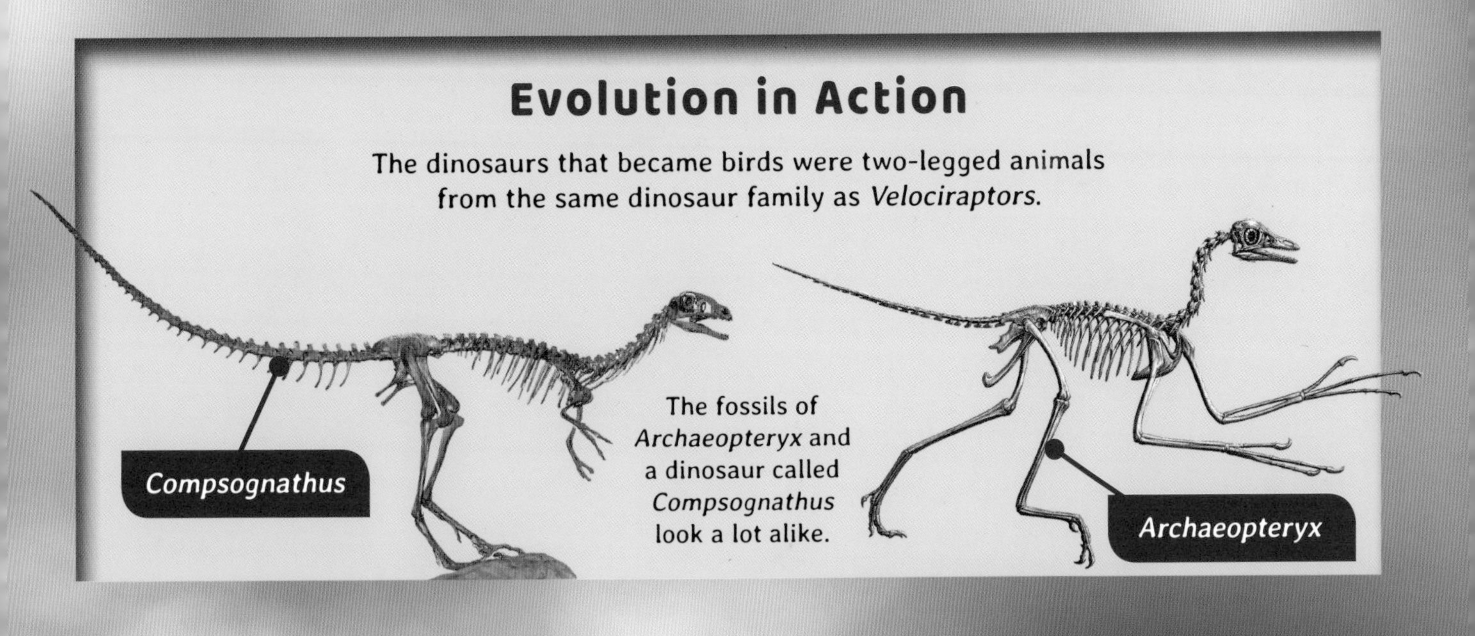

Evolution in Action

The dinosaurs that became birds were two-legged animals from the same dinosaur family as *Velociraptors*.

The fossils of *Archaeopteryx* and a dinosaur called *Compsognathus* look a lot alike.

Robin

Modern birds have toothless beaks. They have no claws on their wings.

Palaeontologists have now found the fossils of many kinds of prehistoric birds. Over time, these birds evolved to have toothless beaks. They also lost their dinosaur-like bony tails and developed tail feathers.

Then, about 66 million years ago, a giant asteroid crashed into Earth. The asteroid caused fires and floods, killing most of the dinosaurs and the prehistoric birds.

Some birds survived, however. They continued to evolve and became the many different species of birds on Earth today!

Keel-billed toucan

Wolves in Our World

It wasn't only dinosaurs that evolved to become new species of animals. Prehistoric dog-like predators evolved and became wolves, coyotes and jackals. But dog evolution didn't stop there!

About 20,000 years ago, some grey wolves began living alongside ancient humans.

Scientists don't know for sure how or where this first happened. Perhaps some wolves overcame their natural fear of humans when they learned that they could find scraps of food around human settlements.

Maybe just like today, people couldn't resist a cute puppy and they captured wild wolf cubs to tame them and keep them as pets.

However it came about, wild grey wolves became the **ancestors** of all the pet and working dogs on Earth. In time, people realised that dogs enjoy attention and can be trained to do work. The evolution of dogs would continue!

Grey wolf

A New Pack?

Wolves live in small family groups, or packs. They hunt as a team and share their food. Ancient wolves were used to living in this way, too. Perhaps this helped them evolve to fit in with a new kind of pack – human families!

Let's Investigate

Crossbreeding Dogs

Over thousands of years, humans have created and bred hundreds of different dog breeds for hunting, protection and companionship. Each breed has physical features, mental abilities and a personality suited to its job.

Border Collies are athletic, energetic and very intelligent. This makes them suitable for sheep herding.

German Shepherds are often used as police dogs due to their strength and extremely protective nature. Their incredible sense of smell can also be used to detect explosive materials or illegal drugs.

Some dogs are crossbred to have desirable features from both parents. Labradors are friendly and intelligent and are often trained to be guide dogs for people who can't see. But what if a blind person is allergic to dogs? Poodles have fur that does not make people with allergies ill. By crossing a Labrador with a poodle, the first sneeze-free labradoodle guide dog was born!

Labrador + Poodle = Labradoodle

What features has the crossbred Pomsky inherited from its parents?

Pomeranian +

Husky = Pomsky

New dog breeds are sometimes named by merging the parents' breed names to create a new name.

Let's Try It

Download our list of dog breeds and get to know some different species of dogs. If you bred two of these different dogs together, what do you think their offspring would look like? Have a go at designing and naming your own crossbreed dog.

Glossary

amphibian
A cold-blooded (ectothermic) vertebrate animal. Most young amphibians live in water and breathe through gills. Adults live on land and in water and breathe air. Frogs, toads, salamanders and caecilians are all amphibians.

ancestor
A relative who lived long ago.

bird
A warm-blooded (endothermic) vertebrate animal with feathers, wings and a beak. All birds lay eggs and most can fly.

carnivore
An animal that eats only meat.

characteristic
A feature that helps to identify something — for example, a characteristic of birds is that they have feathers.

classify
To arrange a group of things, for example animals, according to shared characteristics or features.

cocoon
A case in which some insects change from a larva into a pupa and then into an adult.

cold-blooded
Not able to generate body heat. Cold-blooded animals get their heat from the air or water around them. *Ectothermic* is another word for cold-blooded.

consumer
A living thing that eats other plants, animals or both.

digest
To break down food into substances that can be absorbed into a person or animal's body to give it energy.

energy
The force that allows things to happen. Animals get energy from their food.

evolve
To change little by little over a long period of time.

exoskeleton
The hard outer covering that protects the bodies of insects, spiders and some other invertebrates such as lobsters, crabs and shrimps.

extinct
No longer living; gone forever.

fertilise
To introduce sperm to an egg so it can develop into a new animal.

fish
A cold-blooded (ectothermic) vertebrate animal that lives in water. Fish have scales, gills and fins. Most lay eggs, but some give birth to live young.

fledge
To have grown flight feathers and be ready to leave the nest and fly.

food chain
A series of living things that each get their food (energy) from the living thing that is before them in the chain.

food web
A system of connected food chains or relationships that show the many different ways that animals, plants and other living things get their food in a habitat.

fossilise
To become a fossil. A fossil is the hard remains of a once-living thing that are preserved in rock.

gills
The breathing organs of fish and some amphibians. Gills take oxygen from water, allowing it to pass into the blood.

habitat
The place where a living thing, such as a plant or animal, makes its home.

herbivore
An animal that eats only plants.

incubate
(In birds) To keep an egg warm by sitting on it so that the chick inside grows.

insect
A small invertebrate animal with six legs, a body in three main parts (the head, thorax and abdomen) and a pair of antennae. Most insects have wings.

invertebrate
An animal with no backbone or internal skeleton. Some invertebrates, such as insects or crabs, have an exoskeleton.

larva
The young form of some types of animals. The larvae of insects, for example butterfly caterpillars, usually have long, fat bodies.

mammal
A warm-blooded (endothermic) vertebrate animal with hair or fur. Mammals give birth to live young and feed them milk.

mate
An animal's partner with which it reproduces. Also, a verb (to mate) describing when a male and female animal come together to breed.

microscopic
Visible only through a microscope.

migration
A long journey made by an animal to find food or a mate, or to move from one place to another to avoid cold or hot weather.

nectar
A sweet, sugary liquid produced by plants to attract insects and other animals.

omnivore
An animal that eats both meat and plants.

palaeontologist
A scientist who studies animals and plants from the past.

photosynthesis
The process by which plants make their own food using sunlight, water and carbon dioxide gas.

predator
An animal that hunts and eats other animals.

prey
An animal that is hunted by other animals for food.

producer
A living thing that is able to produce its own food. Plants can produce glucose (a sugary food) in their leaves through photosynthesis.

pupa
The stage in the life cycle of some insects when they change from larvae into adults.

reproduce
To make more of something.

reptile
A cold-blooded (ectothermic) vertebrate animal with scales. Most reptiles lay eggs, but some give birth to live young. Snakes, lizards, alligators, crocodiles, turtles and tortoises are all reptiles.

secrete
To naturally produce and discharge or release a substance.

species
Different types of living things. The members of an animal species look alike and can produce young together.

spider
An invertebrate animal with eight legs and a body in two main parts (the abdomen and the cephalothorax).

territory
An area within an animal's habitat where it finds food or mates. It may defend its territory against others of its species.

vertebrate
An animal with a spine (backbone) made of small bones called vertebrae. Mammals, birds, reptiles, amphibians and fish are all vertebrates.

warm-blooded
Able to generate body heat. *Endothermic* is another word for warm-blooded.

Index

Answers

Page 10:
Every minute about 40,000 tiny bits of dead skin fall off your body. Dust mites feed on this skin, helping to keep our carpets, sofas and beds clean!

Page 11:
All birds have a two-part stomach. In the first part, digestive juices break down their food. The second part is called the gizzard. Some birds that eat hard seeds or nuts also swallow pebbles and sand, which collect in their gizzard. Birds don't have teeth, so the gritty mixture inside the birds' gizzards helps to break up their tough food.